THE TEACHER'S GUIDE
TO USING
FUNDAMENTALS OF PARLIAMENTARY LAW AND PROCEDURE

Fourth Edition

AMERICAN INSTITUTE OF PARLIAMENTARIANS
2014

EDUCATION DEPARTMENT

Jeanette N. Williams, CP-T, Education Director

Ann L. Rempel, CPP-T, Printed Materials Division Chair

© 2014

By American Institute of Parliamentarians

(888) 664-0428

www.aipparl.org

aip@aipparl.org

Produced in the United States of America.

Originally entitled *Parliamentary Law and Procedure Student Workbook*

Fourth Edition ISBN 978-0-942736-40-3
Fourth Edition printed September 2014
1 2 3 4 5 6 7 8 9 10

Produced by the
Education Department
American Institute of Parliamentarians
Jeanette N. Williams, CP-T, Education Director
Ann Rempel, CPP-T, Printed Materials Division Chair
Alison Wallis, CP-T, President

Introduction

The original *Teacher's Guide to using Fundamentals of Parliamentary Law and Procedure*, second edition, was developed by the National Parliamentary Education Project under the direction of Dr. Leo G. Athans, Project Director, and Dr. M. Eugene Bierbaum, Teacher Education Facilitator. The project was sponsored by the William Hearst Foundation to promote parliamentary education classes and programs for the four-year schools of higher learning, community colleges, and select secondary schools. The original *Teacher's Guide* has provided the basis for its successors.

This edition of the *Teacher's Guide* has been updated to accompany the fourth edition (2014) of *Fundamentals of Parliamentary Law and Procedure*. It is a valuable resource for all teachers who use the *Fundamentals* text in their classes.

Part I consists of instructional outlines useful for both classroom and workshop applications. The teaching aids in Part II consist of classroom activities designed to reinforce the learning process. Part III consists of evaluative test questions.

Teachers of parliamentary procedure should utilize the contents of *The Teacher's Guide* with discretion. Use games and exercises to reinforce previously learned concepts, and move on to new concepts only when students have reached the appropriate level of readiness. While questions and answers in the text are excellent for review, the questions in this *Guide* are more appropriate for tests administered at the end of a unit of instruction or for a final examination.

All text references in this Guide are keyed to *Fundamentals of Parliamentary Law and Procedure*, Fourth Edition. Exercises in this Guide are based on *American Institute of Parliamentarians Standard Code of Parliamentary Procedure*, 2012, (*AIPSC*), McGraw-Hill, New York, NY and *Robert's Rules of Order Newly Revised*, Eleventh Edition, 2011, (*RONR*), Da Capo Press, a member of the Perseus Books Group, Philadelphia, PA.

This page intentionally left blank.

CONTENTS

PART I: INSTRUCTIONAL OUTLINES

This page intentionally left blank

PART I. Instructional Outlines

Introduction

The importance of sound structure for teaching beginners cannot be over-emphasized. The teacher should think in terms of a "building blocks" approach in which, if any block of knowledge is omitted, the entire structure falls apart. Principles must be mastered intellectually, one at a time, and then applied. The order in which concepts are taught is essentially outlined in the student's text. However, modifications are necessary to maximize teaching effectiveness within the framework of a given course.

The following outlines illustrate typical learning sequences for three distinctly different course formats: the semester length credit bearing course, the short course, and the single session workshop. All of the outlines are keyed to the student's use of *Fundamentals of Parliamentary Law and Procedure*, Fourth Edition.

It is no accident that the semester length and short course outlines are relatively short, whereas the outline for the single session workshop is much longer. The single session outline contains much more detail, showing specific lecture material and classroom activities.

The teacher of parliamentary procedure should study the format of these outlines, but not slavishly follow the outlines as presented. Effective teachers constantly adapt materials to student needs, including such variables as the size of the class, age level, previous exposure to parliamentary procedure, and the students' immediate and long-range needs. It is unlikely that any teacher will utilize any of outlines as presented, but they should be helpful to providing structure for the learning process.

This page intentionally left blank

Semester Length Credit Bearing Course

Course Objectives

1. To develop an awareness and appreciation of the principles of sound meeting procedures.

2. To develop presiding skills, as well as participation skills, during meetings.

3. To develop skills in composing and amending the governance documents of an organization.

4. To understand the respective roles of officers, boards, committees, and individual members within the organizational structure.

5. To become familiar with resources for continued parliamentary education that are available from American Institute of Parliamentarians (AIP), such as the certification program, texts, correspondence courses, workshops, and practicums.

Class Schedule

Class #	Topic(s)	Reading Assignment*
1.	Basic principles, Order of Business	Lesson 1, 2, 3, 4
2.	Main Motions, Resolutions	Lesson 5, 6
3.	Amending, Precedence of Motions	Lesson 7, 8
4.	Subsidiary Motions	Lesson 9
5.	Privileged Motions	Lesson 10
6.	Incidental Motions	Lesson 11
7.	Changing Previous Decisions	Lesson 12
8.	Debate, Strategy of Debate	Lesson 14, 15
9.	Quorum, Minutes.	Lesson 16, 17
10.	Finances, Membership	Lesson 18, 21
11.	Officers, Executive Board, Parliamentarian	Lesson 13, 19, 20, 30
12.	Committees, Committee Reports	Lesson 22, 23
13.	Bylaws, Standing Rules	Lesson 24, 25, 26
14.	Voting Methods, Nominations, Elections	Lesson 27, 28, 29
15.	Discipline, Conventions	Lesson 31, 32

*TEXT: *Fundamentals of Parliamentary Law and Procedure*, Fourth Edition.

The above course outline assumes fifteen weeks of instruction, one 2½ to 3 hour meeting per week, with additional time for a comprehensive written final examination.

Recommended Classroom Procedure

1. Regular attendance is critical to the student's progress. Student performance in class should be a major part of the student's final grade. Absences necessarily result in reduced student performance. A weak attendance record should trigger penalties against the final grade assigned.

2. In addition to a final written comprehensive examination, short tests (quizzes) may be given frequently and without previous warning. Students are expected to keep up with reading assignments and be prepared to be tested on the material at every class meeting.

3. Students learn more from their own performances than from lengthy lectures. Lectures, as a general rule, should not exceed one-third to one-half of the class period. Early sessions should focus on oral demonstrations. Later class sessions may focus on parliamentary games.

4. A term paper assignment is recommended. Sample term paper assignment: submit a copy of the bylaws of a real organization. Also, submit at least five formal amendments which, if adopted, would improve these bylaws. If required to submit the amendments as resolutions, the "whereas" clauses of the resolutions should state the reasons for the proposed changes; the "resolved" clauses should state the exact wording of the proposed changes. (See Lesson 6 of text for format of resolutions.)

Sample Grading Format*

Class Performance and Attendance	25%
Average Quiz Scores	25%
Term Paper	25%
Final Examination	25%

*__Note:__ The instructor's basis of grading should be clearly explained during the first class meeting, and should be included in the course outline.

Short Course

Course Objectives

1. To develop an awareness of the principles for handling motions during business meetings.

2. To develop presiding skills, as well as participation skills, for business meetings.

3. To develop skills for handling twenty selected motions:

   a. Main Motion

   b. Postpone Indefinitely (*RONR*) or Table (*AIPSC*)

   c. Amend

   d. Refer to Committee

   e. Postpone to a Certain Time

   f. Limit or Extend Debate

   g. Previous Question (Close Debate and Vote Now)

   h. Lay on the Table (*RONR*)

   i. Call for Orders of the Day (*RONR*)

   j. Raise a Question of Privilege (*RONR*), Question of Privilege (*AIPSC*)

   k. Recess

   l. Adjourn

   m. Fix a Time for an Adjourned Meeting (*RONR*)

   n. Appeal

   o. Consideration by Paragraph

   p. Division of a Question

   q. Division of Assembly

   r. Parliamentary Inquiry

   s. Request for Information (*RONR*) or Factual Inquiry (*AIPSC*)

   t. Point of Order

Class Schedule

Class #	Topic(s)	Reading Assignment*
1.	Main motions and amendments	pp. 27-35, 41-51
2.	Precedence of motions. Motions to lay on the table, previous question, limit or extend debate. Individual demonstrations.**	pp. 53-68
3.	Motions to postpone to a certain time, refer to committee, amend, postpone indefinitely. Individual demonstrations.**	pp. 68-79
4.	Motions to fix time, adjourn, recess, question of privilege, orders of the day. Individual demonstrations.**	pp. 81-89
5.	Appeal, consideration by paragraph, division of a question, division of assembly, parliamentary inquiry, request for information, point of order. Script assignment due.***	pp. 91-104

Notes:

* **TEXT: *Fundamentals of Parliamentary Law and Procedure.* Fourth Edition.**

** See Activity #1-Oral Demonstrations in this Teacher's Guide.

*** SCRIPT ASSIGNMENT: Script of the new business portion of a fictitious meeting which correctly utilizes the following motions: main motion, first degree amendment, second degree amendment, motion to commit. The first and second degree amendments must be adopted before voting on the motion to commit.

1. The above course outline assumes five weeks of instruction, one 2½ to 3 hour meeting per week, with additional time for a comprehensive written final examination.

2. Classroom procedures are the same as for the semester length course (see Semester Length Credit Bearing Course in Part I of this Guide) except that a short script assignment is substituted for the term paper.

3. If this is offered as a non-credit course, certificates of achievements may be distributed to those with perfect or near-perfect attendance.

Single Session Workshop: Basic Introduction to Motions

Text Reference

This workshop is designed to utilize Sample Mock Meeting #1 in Appendix B, pp. 286-290.

Lecture Outline

I. Pending Motions

A. A motion is said to be pending after four things have happened in sequence:

1. A member is recognized.

2. A motion is moved.

3. The motion is seconded.

4. The motion is stated by the chair.

B. A motion that is pending loses its status as a pending motion in any of the following ways:

1. The motion is voted on and the result announced.

2. The motion is withdrawn.

3. The motion is temporarily disposed of by such methods as:

   a. Refer to committee.

   b. Postpone to a certain time.

   c. Lay on the table. (*RONR*)

Discussion Questions

- How many motions can be pending at the same time? (infinite)

- How many main motions can be pending at the same time? (one)

- If more than one motion is pending, how does the chair decide which is the "immediately pending question?" (The motion to be voted on first; or, the highest ranking motion)

- How many times can a motion be amended? (infinite)

- How many first degree amendments can be pending at the same time? (one)

- How many second degree amendments can be pending at the same time? (one)

- How many third degree amendments can be pending at the same time? (none)

Summary

The number of times a motion can be amended is unlimited, but:

- Only one main motion can be pending at a time.

- Only one primary amendment can be pending at a time.

- Only one secondary amendment can be pending at a time.

II. Priority versus Standard Recognition.

A.   Standard recognition has two primary characteristics:

  1.   It is hard to get.

     a.   Must wait for it.

     b.   Must yield to any speaker seeking priority recognition.

  2.   Once obtained, the speaker has a wide range of options.

     a.   Ordinary debate, subject to time limits.

     b.   Close debate, amend, refer, postpone, etc.

B.   Priority recognition has two primary characteristics:

  1.   It is easy to get. (Move ahead of other speakers.)

  2.   Once obtained, the speaker has very limited options.

     a.   Whatever occurs must be brief.

     b.   Chair has the obligation to enforce limitations.

C.   Examples of priority recognition and what occurs next:

  1.   Request for Information

     a.   Member needs a fact prior to voting.

     b.   Fact is supplied by the chair or by the chair's designee.

  2.   Point of Order.

     a.   Member cites a procedural error.

     b.   Error is corrected.

  3.   Parliamentary Inquiry.

     a.   Member needs procedural information.

b. Information is supplied by the chair, the parliamentarian or the chair's designee.

4. Call for Division of the Assembly.

a. Member doubts the result of a voice vote.

b. Chair takes a rising uncounted vote.

Note: The most important abuse of priority recognition is that a member may gain priority recognition (which is easy to get) and then proceed to do some of the things (such as debate) that require standard recognition.

Summary:
Priority recognition is easy to get, but then only one thing can be done, and it must be brief. Standard recognition is much more difficult to obtain, but once obtained the speaker has many options.

Scripted Mock Meeting

The scripted mock meeting that begins on page 286 in *Fundamentals,* Fourth Edition, demonstrates both the principle of pending motions and the types of recognition by the chair. Using the procedures for "Fully Scripted Meetings" on page 282, have the class read through the mock meeting on pp. 286-290. At the conclusion of the mock meeting, the following review quiz may be given.

Quiz

1. When does a motion become *pending?*

2. How many times can a motion be amended?

3. How many times can an amendment be amended?

4. How many motions can be pending at the same time?

5. How many amendments can be pending at the same time?

6. What is the difference between a *pending motion* and *the immediately pending question?*

7. List at least three ways that a pending motion may be disposed of.

8. When is it in order to move a secondary amendment?

9. What is the purpose of:

a. a point of order?

b. a parliamentary inquiry?

c. a request for information/factual inquiry?

10. When is it in order to rise to:

    a. a point of order?

    b. a parliamentary inquiry?

    c. a request for information?

11. When is it in order to move to close debate?

12. When is it in order to move to adjourn?

Answers to Quiz

1. A motion becomes pending when it is stated by the chair.

2. The number of times a motion can be amended is infinite, but only one primary and one secondary amendment can be pending at the same time.

3. The number of times an amendment can be amended is infinite, but only one secondary amendment at a time can be pending.

4. There is no limit to the number of motions that can be pending at the same time, provided they are in the correct order of precedence.

5. Two amendments can be pending at the same time, one primary and one secondary.

6. A pending motion has been stated by the chair and is ready to be acted on; however, higher ranking motions may need to be acted on first. The immediately pending question is the first motion to be voted on.

7. A pending motion may be disposed of by:

    a. Adopting or defeating the motion.

    b. Adopting any of the following: postpone indefinitely (*RONR*), refer to a committee, postpone to a certain time, lay on the table (*RONR*), table (*AIPSC*).

    c. Withdrawing the motion.

8. A secondary amendment can be moved whenever a primary amendment is the immediately pending question.

9. The purpose of:

    a. a point of order is to call an error to the chair's attention.

    b. a parliamentary inquiry is to request procedural information.

    c. a request for information is to request factual information about a pending motion.

10.	It is in order to rise to a point of order, a parliamentary inquiry, or a request for information at any time. These motions must be recognized ahead of other motions, and they can interrupt a speaker.

11.	It is in order to move to close debate at any time that a debatable motion is immediately pending; however, this motion requires standard recognition.

12.	It is in order to move to adjourn at any time; however, this motion requires standard recognition.

This page intentionally left blank

PART II: PRACTICAL TEACHING AIDS

This page intentionally left blank

PART II. Practical Teaching Aids

Introduction

The activities approach to parliamentary procedure is based on the premise that the most effective learning occurs in the meeting situation. A major advantage of the activities approach is that it provides many opportunities to learn through trial and error. The student tries to propose a motion and discovers that he cannot say it properly. Or he offers a motion at the wrong time and is ruled out of order. Or he tries out a strategy that backfires, and later learns that his motion could have been adopted if only he had used the correct strategy.

As the student gradually compiles a list of successes and failures in working with different parliamentary strategies, he begins to group his past experiences with various motions into patterns that will govern future strategies. Students who have had positive experiences with raising points of order, for example, are likely to continue this pattern of behavior. Students who have been ruled out of order and have lost an appeal after raising a point of order are likely to abandon this mode of behavior and search for new strategies. The instructor's role is to observe these types of behavior and help the student find acceptable alternative behaviors that will increase effectiveness in a meeting situation.

A second advantage of the activities approach to learning is the emphasis on motivation. A student who knows that he will be dismissed at the end of a lecture may or may not be motivated to listen, depending largely upon the instructor's lecture skills. If, however, the student knows that a quiz will be given at the end of the period, this will somewhat increase the motivation to pay attention. If some of the student's closest friends and relatives are in the same class, and if test scores were to be written on the board and compared (but without names, of course), the level of motivation would be still higher. The highest level of motivation, however, occurs when the student knows in advance that he will be expected to participate in an activity immediately following the lecture. The student's success or failure in the activity depends directly on how much information he gathered from the lecture. Failure to listen and comprehend may result in an embarrassing communication breakdown during the activity period.

A third advantage of the activities approach to learning parliamentary procedure is that students enjoy it. An instructor who deprives students of the sheer fun of learning is missing out on one of the major motivations for effective learning. Students like to experiment and laugh at their own mistakes. They enjoy the involvement of a mock meeting, whether in the role of chair or voting member. Almost any kind of direct involvement through active participation is preferable to the role of passive observer. Perhaps the single most important advantage of activity-based learning is in the area of vocabulary involvement. The reason that students find parliamentary procedure difficult to learn is that they do not feel comfortable with parliamentary terminology. Casual, day-to-day conversation among friends simply does not include such language as "Madam Chair," "Will the speaker yield?" "I second the motion," or "I move the previous question."

The instructor's emphasis, then, must be on the student's spoken language. From this point of view, learning parliamentary procedure is much like learning a foreign language. It is learned by talking, by listening, and by interacting with others in the accepted vocabulary. Most importantly, it is an oral form of communication, and it must be taught orally. Learning occurs only when the student is allowed to "stumble through" some awkward phraseology, make the necessary correction, and try again.

Learning occurs when the student says, "I motion that–," "I amend the motion that--," or "I call for a recess." The instructor instantly recognizes the errors in such statements, but does not ridicule or belittle the effort. With great patience, the instructor states the error and provides the correct language. The student is then invited to try again. Through simple trial and error, plus the added reinforcement of repetition, the student gradually learns how to speak the language of parliamentary procedure. Confidence comes when the student senses the power and influence in the decision making process that is possible through the proper application of parliamentary procedure.

The activities that follow are designed for use with the *Fundamentals of Parliamentary Law and Procedure*, Fourth Edition. Some are targeted specifically at vocabulary development, while others focus on more specialized areas such as seconding motions or preparing a tellers' report. all of them utilize direct student involvement as the primary means of learning. It is recommended that at least 50% to 75% of each class period be devoted to activity based learning. Activities should be carefully supervised, and weak performances should be repeated until the student demonstrates mastery of the desired skills.

ACTIVITY #1: ORAL DEMONSTRATIONS

Text Reference:

Page references are noted separately for each oral demonstration.

Procedures

The oral demonstrations below are patterned after the semi-scripted mock meetings (Sample Partially Scripted Mock Meetings in Appendix B) on p. 283 in *Fundamentals,* Fourth Edition. The purpose of the demonstration is to develop vocabulary. Students should understand that, in addition to mastering the concepts of parliamentary procedure, they must also become proficient in "speaking the language" of parliamentary procedure. The procedures on p. 282-283 in Appendix B are recommended.

In preparing for the demonstrations, the instructor should point out that the "correctness" of each demonstration is practically guaranteed. All roles are assigned in advance, so the presider knows the exact content of each motion and the identity of the mover. The result and effect of each vote is also known in advance. Yet, even with all of this advance knowledge, planning, and rehearsal, beginning presiders will often hesitate, stumble, forget to take the negative vote, ignore the effect of an important vote, incorrectly state the pending question, forget to ask for discussion, improperly recognize speakers, and so forth. These common errors provide an opportunity for the instructor to emphasize the importance of **practice** in developing presiding skills.

The point of these demonstrations is to develop **fluency** in presiding. Demonstrations should be timed, and should be repeated as often as necessary to cut down the amount of time consumed by awkward pauses and hesitations as well as time spent in correcting procedural errors. Repeat each demonstration until it moves along smoothly with minimal nonfluencies and hesitations.

Oral Demonstrations (most are based on *RONR*)

1. A offers a main motion. B moves to amend the main motion by striking out and inserting words. The amendment and the main motion are adopted. (pp. 27-31, 41-45)

2. A offers a main motion. B moves to amend by adding words. C moves to amend the amendment by striking out and inserting words. All votes are in the affirmative. (pp. 42-43)

3. A offers a main motion. After brief discussion, B moves to refer the main motion to a committee of three to be appointed by the chair. The motion to refer is adopted. The chair appoints the committee, naming the committee chairman first. (pp. 70-72)

4. A offers a main motion. B moves to postpone the main motion indefinitely. C moves to amend the main motion by striking out words. The amendment is defeated; the motion to postpone indefinitely is adopted. (pp.73-74)

5. A offers a main motion. B moves to postpone the main motion until the next regular meeting. C moves to amend by striking out the "regular." The amendment and the motion to postpone are defeated. The main motion is adopted. (pp. 68-69)

6. A offers a main motion. After brief discussion, B moves to limit debate to one minute per speech. C moves to amend by striking out "one" and inserting "two." D, explaining that an urgent matter has arisen, moves to lay the main motion on the table. The motion to lay on the table is defeated. All remaining motions are adopted. (pp. 63-64, 66-68)

7. A offers a main motion. B moves to refer the main motion to a committee of five to be elected. C moves to amend by striking out "five" and inserting "three." D moves the previous question. All motions that are put to a vote are adopted. The chair announces that an election will now take place. (pp. 65-66)

8. A offers a main motion. B moves to postpone discussion of the main motion for one week. C moves to amend the motion by striking out "one week" and inserting "two weeks." D moves the previous question. Before the chair can put the previous question to a vote, E moves the previous question on all pending questions. All motions put to a vote are adopted. (pp. 65-66, 68-69)

9. A offers a main motion. B moves a substitute motion. The substitute is adopted. (pp. 43-44)

10. A offers a main motion. B, explaining that an urgent matter has arisen, moves to lay the main motion on the table. C moves to recess for ten minutes. D moves to adjourn. All motions, when put to a vote, are defeated except the main motion, which is adopted. (pp. 63-64, 82-84)

11. A offers a main motion. B moves to amend by striking out and inserting words. C moves to adjourn. D moves to fix the time to which to adjourn. C moves to amend the motion to fix time. All motions that are voted on are adopted. (p. 82)

12. A offers a motion containing two distinct parts. After brief discussion, B moves to divide the question. The motion to divide the question is adopted, and the first part of the question is adopted. The second part, when voted on, is defeated. (pp. 95-97)

13. A offers a main motion that appears to be absurd in content. B objects to consideration of the motion. The chair puts the question of consideration to a vote and a majority, but fewer than two-thirds, vote against consideration of the main motion. C moves to amend the main motion. The amendment and the main motion are adopted. (pp. 94-95)

14. A offers a main motion. B moves to amend by adding words. C moves to amend the amendment by striking out words. D moves to refer the main motion to the finance committee. E moves to amend the motion to refer by adding a date for the committee to report back. After brief discussion, the chair takes the vote on the amendment to the motion to refer. The chair announces that the amendment is adopted, but F calls out "Division!" The chair takes the division of the assembly, and the amendment is defeated. The motion to refer is adopted. (pp. 97-98)

15. A offers a main motion. B offers a motion to commit. C moves to limit debate to 20 minutes. The motion to limit debate is adopted. After brief debate, D moves the previous question. The vote on the previous question is exactly two-thirds in the affirmative and exactly one-third in the negative. The chair votes in the negative and the previous question is defeated. After brief discussion, voting continues, and all motions put to a vote are adopted. (pp. 65-66, 340 Answer #5)

16. A offers a main motion. B moves an amendment which is questionably germane to the main motion. The chair rules the amendment out of order, stating that it is not germane to the main motion. C appeals the decision of the chair. The vote on the appeal results in a tie vote, and the decision of the chair is sustained. The main motion is adopted. (pp. 42, 92-93)

17. A offers a main motion. B moves to postpone the main motion indefinitely. C raises a question of privilege. The chair rules that the question of privilege is to be entertained immediately, and the vote on the question of privilege is in the affirmative. The motion to postpone indefinitely is adopted. (pp. 73-74, 84-85)

18. A moves that our next meeting be held on February 3rd. B moves to amend by striking out February 3rd and creating a blank. B's motion is adopted. Suggestions for filling the blank are then offered by various members of the assembly as follows: March 15, February 10, April 12, and February 1. These are voted on, using *AIPSC* procedure described on p. 46. The blank is filled by inserting February 10, and the amended main motion is adopted. (pp. 45-46)

19. A main motion "to invite President Clark to our next meeting" is pending. There has been extensive debate on the motion, but no vote.

A seeks recognition by the chair, and the chair rules that A has already spoken twice and cannot speak a third time. B moves to suspend the rule which prohibits a member from speaking more than twice. The chair announces that a two-thirds vote will be required to suspend the rule for reasons stated on p. 94. The motion to suspend the rule is adopted. Discussion continues, and the main motion is adopted. (pp. 93-94)

20.   A offers a main motion and, after brief discussion, the motion is adopted with C voting in the affirmative. B moves to recess for ten minutes, and this motion is adopted. Following the recess, C moves to reconsider the vote on the main motion. The motion to reconsider is adopted; the main motion is defeated. (pp. 84, 109-110)

21.   At a later session, A moves to renew the motion that was defeated in demonstration #20 above. The motion is adopted. B moves to amend the adopted motion, and the amendment is adopted. (pp. 105-106)

22.   A offers a main motion. B, stating that an urgent matter has arisen, moves to lay the main motion on the table. The motion to lay on the table is adopted. C moves to fix the time to which to adjourn, and this is adopted. D moves to take the main motion from the table, and this is adopted. E moves to amend the main motion. The amendment is adopted; the main motion is defeated. (pp. 63-64, 72-73, 82, 108-109)

23.   A moves to rescind the motion that was adopted in demonstration #21 above. The motion to rescind is adopted. B moves to adjourn, and this is adopted. (pp. 82-84, 106-107)

24.   A offers a main motion which can be divided into two parts. B moves to divide the motion into two parts, and the division of the question is adopted. The first part of the main motion is defeated with C voting in the negative. The second part of the main motion is adopted. C moves to reconsider the vote on the first part of the main motion. The motion to reconsider is adopted; the main motion is defeated. (pp. 95-97, 109-110)

ACTIVITY #2: CHAIRING A MEETING

Text Reference:

This game is a variation of the unscripted mock meetings described on pp. 284-285, Appendix B, in *Fundamentals,* Fourth Edition.

Procedures

1. Divide the class into groups of six to eight students.

2. Each group prepares an agenda for the "New Business" portion of a meeting, and the agenda is approved by the instructor. The agenda should contain specific wording for several main motions.

3. The performing group is seated at the front of the room, with all others seated in the rear of the room.

4. Persons who are not in the performing group may not make or discussion motions and are limited to raising points of order and voting on motions.

5. Members of the performing group are responsible for adhering to the adopted agenda. They may propose any motions that are relevant to the agenda.

6. Members of the performing group are in complete control of both motions moved and discussion of the motions. Voting, however, is largely controlled by participants who are not members of the performing group. Members of the performing group must be alert to the changing parliamentary situation as determined by the results of votes taken. They must also be prepared to rotate the chair without notice.

7. The instructor randomly rotates members of the performing group in and out of the chair. Every four to five minutes, without warning, the instructor calls out the name of a new chair. The person going out of the chair returns to become an active member of the performing group. The person coming into the chair immediately continues the meeting where it was left by the outgoing chair.

8. The instructor grades members of the performing group individually, taking into consideration both the correctness of procedures and the level of difficulty of the material attempted.

This page intentionally left blank

ACTIVITY #3 SECONDING MOTIONS

Text Reference:

Lessons 8, 9, 10, 11, and 12.

Procedures

1. Two teams, Team A and Team B, of four or five members are selected to compete in front of the class.

2. Two scorekeepers keep track of the score for each team on the chalkboard.

3. The instructor reads aloud one motion from the "Second or No Second" list below, and allows Team A to respond. A second from any member of the group counts as a second for the entire group. Complete silence from the group counts as no second.

4. The above procedure is repeated for Team B. The scorekeepers at the board write down the answers for Team A and Team B. They mark "S" for second or "N" for no second.

5. Each group's responses to all fifteen motions are recorded on the board. When finished, the class participates in the grading. Discuss each item separately.

6. List of motions:

    a. Point of order.

    b. I rise to a question of privilege.

    c. I move to lay the motion on the table.

    d. I object to consideration of the question.

    e. I appeal the decision of the chair.

    f. I rise to a parliamentary inquiry.

    g. I call for the orders of the day.

    h. I move to reconsider and enter on the minutes.

    i. I move to divide the question into two parts.

    j. Division!

    k. I move the previous question.

    l. I move that this meeting be adjourned in one hour.

    m. Request for information.

n.   I question the presence of a quorum.

o.   I move to recess for ten minutes for the purpose of obtaining a quorum.

7.   Correct responses: #3, 5, 8, 9, 11, 12, 15 require a second. All others should be marked "N."

8.   Keep the same two teams for responding to "What does the chair say next?"

9.   The instructor directs a situation from the list below to a particular individual on Team A. The individual must then give the exact words to be spoken by the chair. The instructor immediately announces whether the response is correct.

10.   The instructor then directs a different situation from the list below to a particular individual on Team B. The individual must give the exact words to be spoken by the chair, and the procedure is repeated.

11.   Scorekeepers at the board score separately for each team. Scores for the two games are added together to determine the winning team.

12.   Questions and answers for "What does the chair say next?"

a.   The chair states the question on a motion. The seconder of the motion then requests permission to withdraw his second. (Ans: It is too late to withdraw a second unless permission is granted by the assembly.)

b.   A committee chair reads his report aloud. It contains a recommendation. After reading the report and moving adoption of the recommendation, the committee chair asks if there is a second for the recommendation. (Ans: Motions from committees of more than one member do not require seconds.)

c.   A main motion is moved. The chair asks if there is a second, but there is no response. (Ans: The motion dies for lack of a second.)

d.   A main motion is moved and seconded. Before the chair states the question, the mover asks permission to change the wording of the motion. (Ans: It is in order for the mover to modify the wording of the motion; however, the seconder may withdraw his second.)

e.   A main motion is moved and seconded. Before the chair states the question, the mover asks permission to withdraw the motion. (Ans: It is in order for the mover to withdraw the motion.

The motion may then be moved by the seconder or any other member.)

f.   A main motion is adopted. Later in the meeting, a member claims that the motion was never seconded. (Ans: It is too late to object to the lack of a second.)

g.   A main motion is moved. Several members simultaneously say "Second." (Ans: The chair immediately states the question on the motion.)

h.   During approval of the minutes, a member complains that he had seconded a motion but the second is omitted from the minutes. (Ans: Second should not be recorded in the minutes.)

i.   Notice of a proposed bylaw amendment was given at the previous meeting, a member moves adoption of the bylaw amendment, and the chair states the question on the amendment as pending. A member states that the amendment was not seconded. (Ans: The chair asks for a second.)

j.   During a committee meeting, a motion is moved, and the chair states the question. A member states that the motion was not seconded. (Ans: Seconds are not required in committees.)

This page intentionally left blank

ACTIVITY #4: TELLERS COMMITTEE (based on *RONR*)

Text Reference:
Lesson 29.

Procedures

1. Divide the class into several groups of four to six students. Each group acts as a tellers committee. All sets of ballots are identical; give one set of twenty-four ballots to each committee. also give one Tellers' Report form to each committee.

2. Each committee elects its own chairman of tellers and develops its own procedure for counting ballots.

3. Allow fifteen to twenty minutes for the committee to count their ballots and prepare a tellers' report.

4. When time is up, each chairman of tellers rises and reads the committee's report. It is important that all committee reports be read aloud before any discussion is permitted. Everyone should listen attentively to the reports and note any apparent errors.

5. After all reports have been heard, lead discussion. Focus on the following:

   a. Why were all reports not the same? (Remind the class that ballots for each committee were identical.)

   b. Did any of the reports contain errors? What were they?

   c. What is meant by the term *majority vote*?

   d. What is the difference between an abstention and an illegal vote?

   e. Discuss several types of illegal votes.

   f. Can a marked ballot ever be considered an abstention? Under what circumstances?

BALLOT FOR THE OFFICE
OF THE PRESIDENT

Nominees: Susan White, Ted Moore, Alice Jones

Situation: According to the bylaws, all persons except the three nominated are ineligible for the office of president. Twenty-four voting members are present, and a ballot vote is taken. Blank ballots are distributed with instructions to write the name of one candidate to be voted for.

Ballots: The table below lists the contents of the twenty-four ballots to be used in this exercise.

Solution to Tellers Committee Game

It is important that this report be read **aloud** by each chairman of tellers before discussion is permitted. Any attempt to announce the result is an error since the presiding officer must declare candidates elected.

Report of the Tellers Committee

Number of votes cast:	21
Number necessary for election:	11

For the Office of President:

Susan White	6
Ted Moore	2
Alice Jones	12
Illegal Votes:	
Bill Evans (ineligible)	1

Note: Three ballots indicated no preference, and therefore were not included in the final tally. One was blank; one was marked "abstain;" and one was marked "Any candidate is o-k."

BALLOT MARKINGS

S. White	Alice Jones	Susan White
A. Jones	Alice J.	Abstain
T. Moore	Susan W.	A. Jones
Alice Jones	Alice J.	
Bill Evans	A. Jonesey	Alice J.
Sue White	Ted M.	Al Jones
Alice Jones	Any candidate o-k	Susan White
A. Jones	Sue White	A. Jons

ACTIVITY #5: Drills on Motions.

Procedures:

1. Display Visual Aid #8 (Drill on Motions) in this Guide on the chalkboard or flip chart, or by projection on a screen.

2. Do a brief oral review for each motion displayed: main motion, postpone definitely, lay on the table, take from the table, and reconsider.

3. Announce that everyone is to serve as temporary secretary by keeping an up-to-date record of which motions are pending, adopted, defeated, or laid on the table.

4. Announce that each student will be responsible for responding orally to at least one parliamentary situation. Nineteen situations are presented; therefore, if there are nineteen students, each student will respond once; if there are six students, each student will respond three times, etc. The instructor may increase or decrease the number of situations to fit the class size prior to starting the drills.

5. The only motions in order are the motions listed on the visual aid, and the exact wording displayed for each motion must be used.

6. After the instructor has read the brief text for a situation, the assigned student must respond by saying the exact words to be spoken by the chair.

7. For an undebatable motion, the student should state the question by saying, "Are you ready for the question?" For a debatable motion, the student should say, "Is there any debate on the motion?" In no case will actual discussion occur. The vote should be taken immediately after the question is stated on the motion.

8. Correct responses are listed following each situation. These answers should be available only to the instructor, who reads the correct response immediately after each student has responded orally. Brief discussion of the adequacy or inadequacy of the student response may ensue prior to moving on to the next situation.

9. The instructor may interrupt the proceedings from time to time to review the status of all motions that have come before the body up to that point. The final status of all motions is given at the end of the exercise.

SITUATION #1:	A member moves that dues be raised to $20.00 per year, effective next January 1. The motion is seconded.
	ANS: (It is moved and seconded that dues be raised to $20.00 per year, effective next January 1. Is there any debate on the motion?)
SITUATION #2:	A member moves to postpone the main motion indefinitely. The motion is seconded.
	ANS: (It is moved and seconded to postpone the main motion indefinitely. Is there debate on the motion to postpone indefinitely?)
SITUATION #3:	A member moves to amend the main motion by striking out the words "effective next January 1" so that the main motion, if amended, would read "that dues be raised to $20.00 per year." The amendment is seconded.
	ANS: (It is moved and seconded to amend the main motion by striking out the words "effective next January 1." If the amendment is adopted, the main motion will be "That dues be raised to $20 per year." Is there any debate on the amendment?)
SITUATION #4:	A member moves to postpone the pending questions until 9:30 p.m. at the next meeting. The motion is seconded.
	ANS: (It is moved and seconded to postpone the pending questions until 9:30 p.m. at the next meeting. Is there any debate on the motion to postpone?)
SITUATION #5:	A member, stating that our guest speaker must depart soon, moves to lay the pending questions on the table. The motion is seconded.
	ANS: (It is moved and seconded to lay the pending questions on the table. . Are you ready for the question? Those in favor of laying the pending questions on the table, say "Aye." Those opposed, say "No.")
SITUATION #6:	The vote on the pending motion is 9 in favor and 7 opposed.
	ANS:(The main motion is laid on the table by a vote of 9-7. Our guest speaker is _____.)

SITUATION #7:   A member moves that membership cards be issued to members upon receipt of dues payment. The motion is seconded.

ANS: (It is moved and seconded that membership cards be issued to members upon receipt of dues payment. Is there any debate on the motion? [Pause.] Those in favor of the motion, say "Aye." Those opposed, say "No.")

SITUATION #8:   The vote on the pending motion is 3 in favor and 11 opposed.

ANS: (The motion is lost by a vote of 3-11. Is there any new business?)

SITUATION #9:   A member moves to take from the table the motions related to raising the dues. The motion is seconded.

ANS: (It is moved and seconded to take from the table the motions related to raising the dues. Are you ready for the question?)

SITUATION #10:   A member moves to reconsider the vote on the motion that membership cards be issued to members upon receipt of dues payment. The motion is seconded.

ANS: (How did the member vote on the original motion? Since the member voted in the negative and the motion was defeated, the motion to reconsider is in order. It is moved and seconded to reconsider the vote on the main motion that membership cards be issued to members upon receipt of dues payment. This motion to reconsider may be called up when no other motion is pending. We will now vote on whether to take from the table the motions related to raising the dues. Those in favor of the motion to take from the table, say "Aye." Those opposed, say "No.")

SITUATION #11:   The vote on the pending motion is 11 in favor and 8 opposed.

ANS: (The motion to take from the table the motions related to raising the dues is adopted by a vote of 11-8. The motions now pending are:

1. Postpone until 9:30 p.m. at the next meeting.

2. Amend by striking out "effective next January 1."

3. Postpone indefinitely.

Is there any debate on the motion to postpone consideration of the question until 9:30 p.m. at the next meeting? [Pause.] Those in favor of postponing consideration of the question until 9:30 p.m. at the next meeting, say "Aye." Those opposed. say "No.")

SITUATION #12:   The vote on the pending motion is 8 in favor and 12 opposed.

ANS: (The motion to postpone consideration of the question until 9:30 p.m. at the next meeting is defeated, 8-12. Is there any debate on the motion to amend the main motion by striking out the words "effective next January 1"? [Pause.] Those in favor of the amendment, say "Aye." Those opposed, say "No.")

SITUATION #13:   The vote on the pending motion 7 in favor and 9 opposed.

ANS: (The amendment is defeated by a vote of 7-9. Is there any debate on the motion to postpone indefinitely? [Pause.] Those in favor of indefinite postponement of the main motion that dues be raised to $20.00 per year, effective next January 1, say "Aye." Those opposed, say "No.")

SITUATION #14:   The vote on the pending motion is 6 in favor and 10 opposed.

ANS: (The motion to postpone indefinitely is defeated, 6-10. Is there any debate on the main motion that dues be raised to $20.00 per year, effective next January 1? [Pause.] Those in favor of the main motion, say "Aye." Those opposed, say "No.")

SITUATION #15:   The vote on the pending motion is 8 in favor and 12 opposed.

ANS: (The main motion is defeated by a vote of 8-12. Is there further new business?)

SITUATION #16:   The mover of the motion to reconsider calls up the motion to reconsider.

ANS: (The pending motion is to reconsider the vote on the main motion, previously defeated, that membership cards be issued to members upon receipt of dues payment. Is there any debate on the motion to reconsider?

Pause. Those in favor of the motion to reconsider, say "Aye." Those opposed, say "No.")

SITUATION #17:   The vote on the pending motion is 10 in favor and six opposed.

ANS: (The motion to reconsider is adopted, 10-6. Is there any debate on the pending main motion that membership cards be issued to members upon receipt of dues payment? [Pause.] Those in favor of the motion, say "Aye." Those opposed, say "No.")

SITUATION #18:   The vote on the pending motion is 10 in favor and 6 opposed.

ANS: (The motion is adopted, and membership cards will be issued to members upon receipt of dues payment. Is there any further new business?)

SITUATION #19:   What motions are now pending?

ANS: (None.)

This page intentionally left blank

Visual Aids

This page intentionally left blank

Visual Aids

Effective teachers recognize the importance of helping their students to **visualize** concepts. When preparing visual aids, do not try to "cram" a great deal of information onto a single visual aid. The ideal visual aid contains a single concept that is easily grasped at a glance. Simplicity and clarity are essential. With practice, the teacher can quickly construct visual aids that help the student "see" how parliamentary procedure works. The eight visual aids presented on the following pages are adaptable to a chalkboard, a flip chart, poster board, or projection on a screen.

Visual Aids #1 and #2 (Main Motion, Agenda) illustrate how simple listings of points contained in the text can help the teacher present concepts during a lecture. Visual Aid #3 (Resolution) illustrates how form can be separated from content to help the student visualize how a resolution should look. Visual Aids #4 and #5 (Types of Amendments) illustrate how simple concepts can be followed up with concrete examples. Visual Aids #6 and #7 (Amending Process, Precedence) illustrate how these concepts can be taught by a "visual laddering technique." Visual Aid #8 (Drill on Motions) illustrates how the laddering technique can be applied to a specific classroom activity.

Using the simple techniques illustrated on the following pages, the teacher can quickly develop visual aids that greatly enhance the quality of a lecture presentation. The laddering technique, illustrated by Visual Aids #6, #7, and #8, is especially useful for teaching the principle of precedence and the processing of motions.

The page references for the Visual Aids are keyed to ***Fundamentals of Parliamentary Law and Procedure***, Fourth Edition.

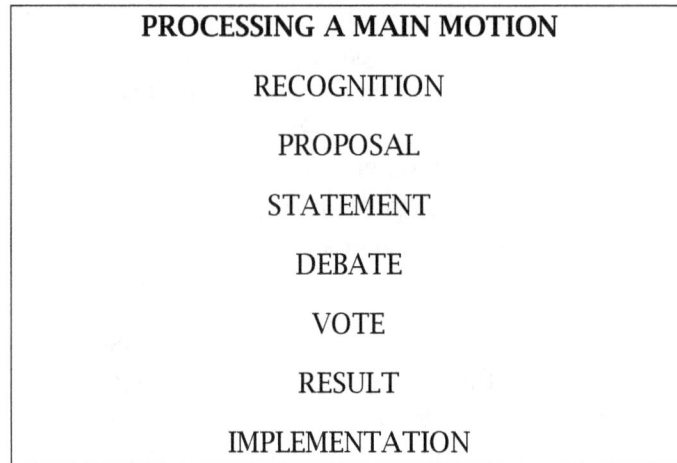

Text: pp. 29-30.

AGENDA

CALL TO ORDER

APPROVAL OF MINUTES

REPORTS:

--OFFICERS

--BOARDS

--STANDING COMMITTEES

--SPECIAL COMMITTEES

SPECIAL ORDERS

UNFINISHED BUSINESS AND GENERAL ORDERS

NEW BUSINESS

ANNOUNCEMENTS

PROGRAM

ADJOURNMENT

Text: pp. 20-23.

RESOLUTION
Whereas, There are no . . . .;
Whereas, The cost of . . . .; and
Whereas, The need for . . . .
. . . . .is significant; therefore be it
Resolved, That . . . . and be it further
Resolved, That . . . .

Text: p. 38.

TYPES OF AMENDMENTS
ADDING WORDS
INSERTING WORDS
STRIKING OUT WORDS
STRIKING OUT AND INSERTING WORDS
SUBSTITUTION

Text: pp. 42-43.

TYPES OF AMENDMENTS

MAIN MOTION:

To pay all expenses for three delegates to attend the state convention in April.

ADD:

Add "if funds are available" after "April."

INSERT:

Insert "elected" between "three" and "delegates."

STRIKE OUT:

Strike out "all."

STRIKE OUT AND INSERT:

Strike out "three delegates" and insert "one delegate."

SUBSTITUTE:

Substitute the following for the entire motion: "To encourage all of our members to attend the state convention in April, and to reimburse travel expenses up to $50 per person."

Text: pp. 42-43.

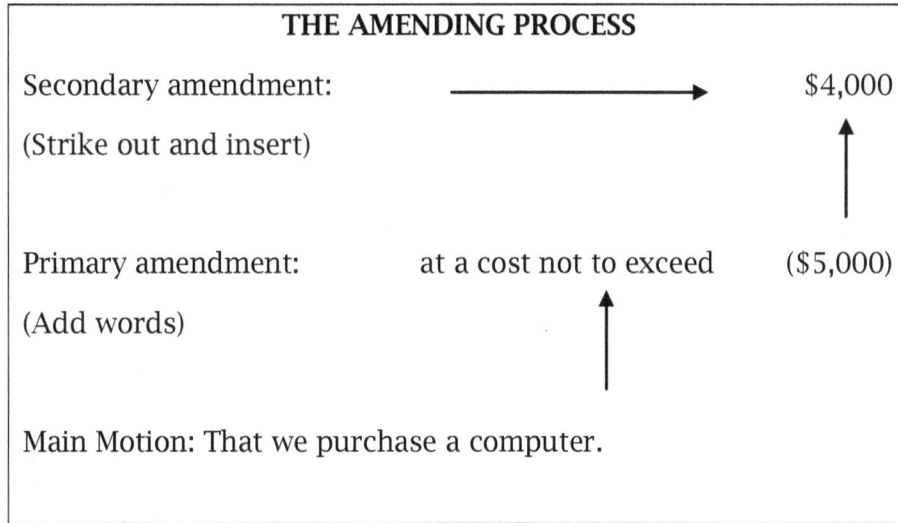

THE AMENDING PROCESS

Secondary amendment: ⟶ $4,000

(Strike out and insert)

Primary amendment: at a cost not to exceed ($5,000)

(Add words)

Main Motion: That we purchase a computer.

Text: p. 43.

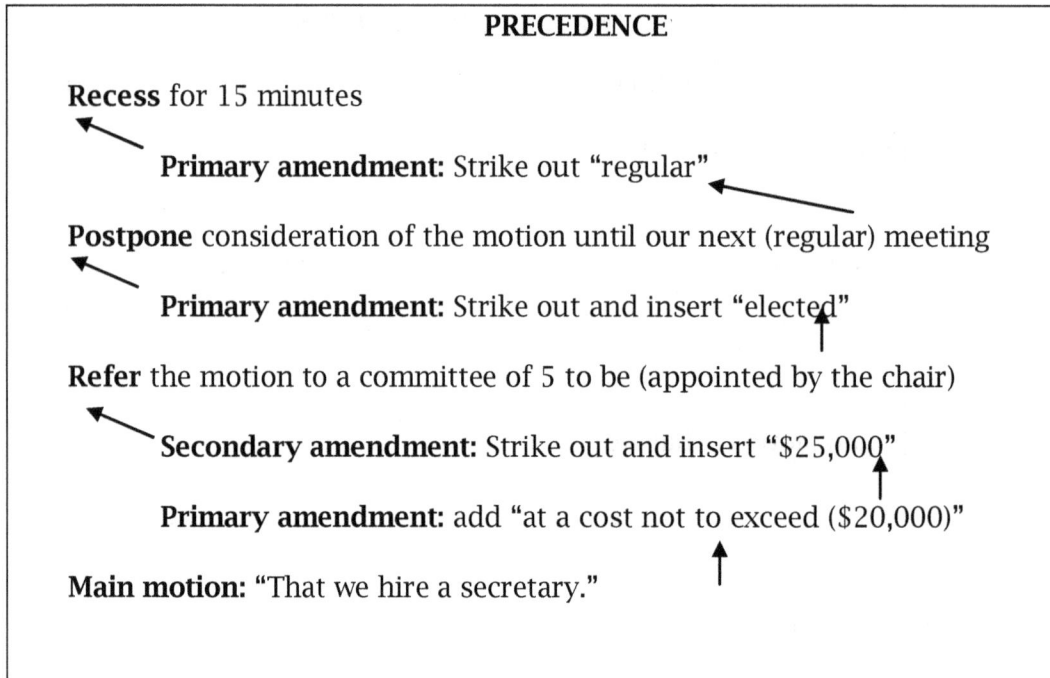

PRECEDENCE

Recess for 15 minutes

    Primary amendment: Strike out "regular"

Postpone consideration of the motion until our next (regular) meeting

    Primary amendment: Strike out and insert "elected"

Refer the motion to a committee of 5 to be (appointed by the chair)

    Secondary amendment: Strike out and insert "$25,000"

    Primary amendment: add "at a cost not to exceed ($20,000)"

Main motion: "That we hire a secretary."

Text: p. 55.

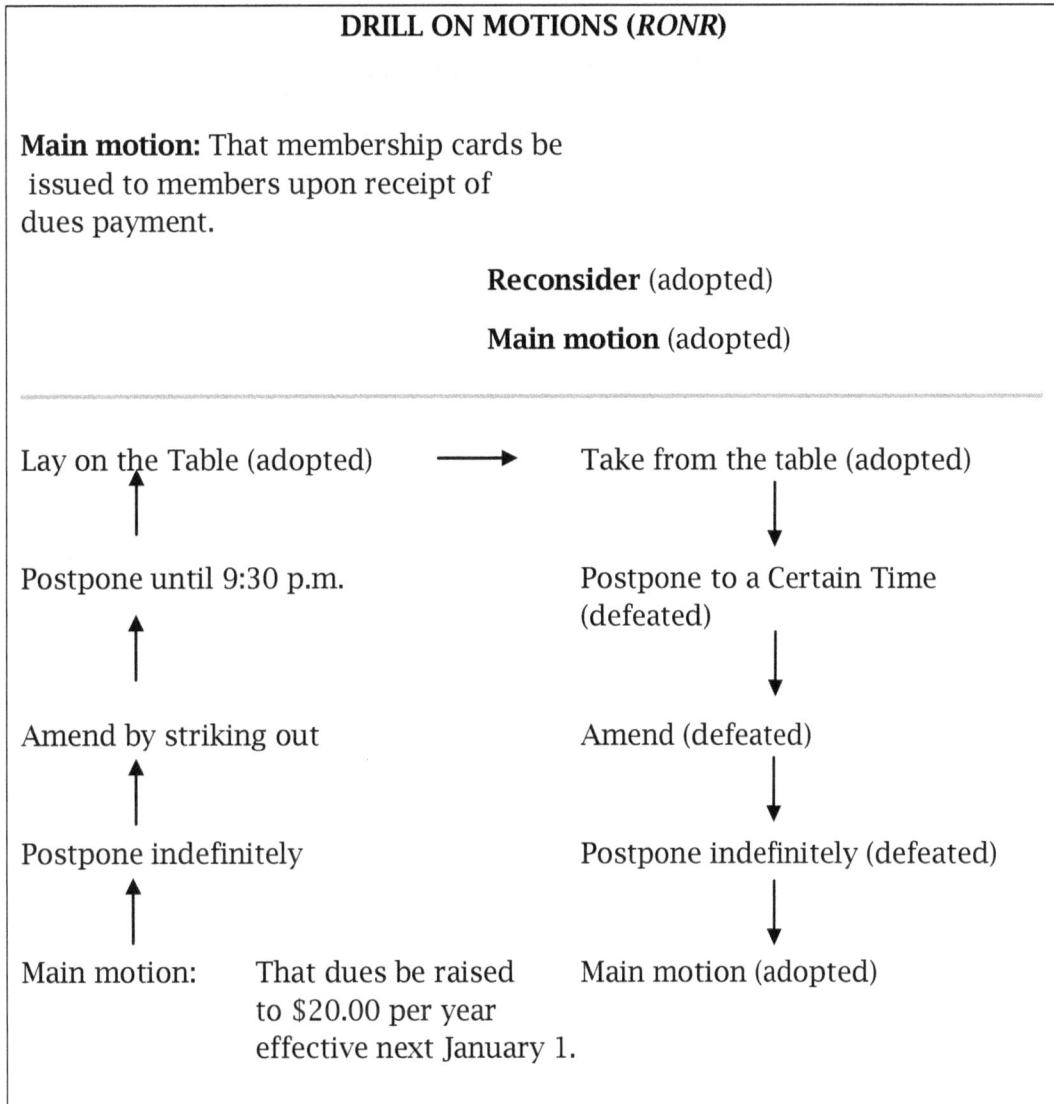

DRILL ON MOTIONS (*RONR*)

Main motion: That membership cards be
issued to members upon receipt of
dues payment.

> **Reconsider** (adopted)
>
> **Main motion** (adopted)

Lay on the Table (adopted) ⟶ Take from the table (adopted)

Postpone until 9:30 p.m.   Postpone to a Certain Time (defeated)

Amend by striking out   Amend (defeated)

Postpone indefinitely   Postpone indefinitely (defeated)

Main motion: That dues be raised to $20.00 per year effective next January 1.   Main motion (adopted)

Text: p. 55.

This page intentionally left blank

PART III. TEST QUESTIONS

This page intentionally left blank

PART III. Test Questions:

Introduction

The test questions on the following pages are very different from the review questions in the text, and they are intended for a different purpose. The questions in the text are review questions, and they are intended for just that purpose: review. The questions presented here are different in two respects; they are more difficult and they are all in the multiple choice format with five possible answers.

It is recommended that the review questions in the text be used primarily for teaching purposes, with ongoing review throughout all class sessions. The questions on the following pages should be used primarily for evaluation and grading purposes. It is strongly recommended, of course, that the questions and answers not be made available to students prior to actual evaluation.

The following 150 test questions cover all thirty-two lessons in the text, with at least two questions and no more than ten questions per lesson. Following each question, the correct answer is given in parenthesis.

Lesson 1: Principles and Rules of Parliamentary Law

1.   A basic principle of order is that:
    A.   All members have equal rights, responsibilities, obligations and privileges.
    B.   No officers have the right to dictate or control decisions unless the members grant such rights.
    C.   All members have the right to be informed, to ask questions, and to have complex motions clarified.
    D.   Only one substantive motion may be pending at one time.
    E.   Only one motion may be pending at one time.   (D)

2.   According to parliamentary law, the most important right of the minority is the right:
    A.   to be informed,
    B.   to serve on committees or as officers.
    C.   to be heard.
    D.   to prevail.
    E.   to sabotage majority decisions.   (C)

3.   A basic principle of justice is that:
    A.   All members have equal rights, responsibilities, obligations, and privileges.
    B.   No members, board, or officers have the right to dictate or control decisions.
    C.   Members are expected to accept the will of the majority.
    D.   The presiding officer must protect members from unfair treatment or abuse.
    E.   Members have the right to be informed, to ask questions, and to have complex motions clarified by the chair.   (E)

Lesson 2: Deliberative Assemblies

1. The primary purpose of an executive session is to:
    A. adopt an annual budget.
    B. conduct a disciplinary hearing.
    C. amend the bylaws.
    D. protect the confidentiality of proceedings.
    E. allow members to attend those meetings which are deemed most important to the welfare of the association.   (D)

2. An adjourned meeting is a meeting that:
    A. adjourns before all of the regularly scheduled business has been completed.
    B. adjourns without providing for a future meeting.
    C. provides for a continuance of the same meeting.
    D. provides for an unscheduled meeting held at a time specified in the call to meeting.
    E. adjourns whenever a quorum is no longer present.   (C)

3. The business of special meetings consists of:
    A. any business within the adopted objects or jurisdiction of the society.
    B. organizing a new society.
    C. a continuance of the business of the previous meeting.
    D. only the business that remains unfinished from a regular meeting.
    E. only the business stated in the call of the meeting.   (E)

4. When a mass meeting is called for the purpose of organizing,
    A. the sponsors have the right to exclude persons who are not in sympathy with the purpose of the meeting.
    B. the meeting must be open to the general public.
    C. those present have the right to debate but not to vote.
    D. a quorum is established only after members have paid dues.
    E. the meeting is limited to general discussion since none of the persons present have membership rights.   (A)

Lesson 3: Organizing a Society

1. When organizing a new society, the group elects permanent officers:
   A. prior to adoption of the bylaws.
   B. immediately following the adoption of a resolution to form a society.
   C. immediately following the enrollment of members.
   D. immediately following the adoption of bylaws.
   E. at any time prior to adjournment of the first meeting.   (C)

2. Organizing a new society generally requires:
   A. one meeting.
   B. two meetings.
   C. at least three meetings.
   D. about six months.
   E. no meetings, since this can be done by mail.   (B)

3. The essential steps required to organize a new society are:
   A. adoption of bylaws, election of officers, and enrollment of members.
   B. adoption of a resolution to form a society, adoption of bylaws, and election of officers.
   C. adoption of a resolution to form a society, election of officers, and enrollment of members.
   D. adoption of a resolution to form a society, adoption of bylaws, and enrollment of members.
   E. adoption of bylaws, election of officers, and appointment of standing committees.   (D)

Lesson 4: Order of Business and Agenda

1. Items are removed from a consent agenda:
    A. only when there is unanimous approval to do so.
    B. when a majority of the members vote to do so.
    C. following a two-thirds affirmative vote.
    D. upon request of any member.
    E. under no circumstances. (D)

2. Call to order, business stated in the call to meeting, and adjournment is a typical order of business for:
    A. a regular meeting.
    B. a special meeting.
    C. an adjourned meeting.
    D. an annual meeting.
    E. a mass meeting. (B)

3. Business that must be considered before unfinished business is:
    A. new business.
    B. a special meeting.
    C. special order of business.
    D. announcements.
    E. the complete adopted agenda. (C)

4. The agenda for organizations that meet frequently is:
    A. open to debate, but not to amendment.
    B. open to amendment, but not to debate.
    C. open both to debate and amendment.
    D. usually placed in the standing rules.
    E. subject to arbitrary amendment by the chair. (D)

5. A program should usually occur:
    A. prior to the call to order.
    B. immediately following the call to order.
    C. following adjournment of the meeting.
    D. immediately prior to adjournment of the meeting.
    E. at the time recommended by the program committee. (D)

Lesson 5: Main Motion

1. Modifications accepted by the maker of a motion may be made:
   A. only before the motion is stated by the chair.
   B. only after the motion is stated by the chair.
   C. either before or after the motion is stated by the chair.
   D. only by adopting amendments to the main motion.
   E. whenever it is clear that the modifications will help to clarify the intent of the main motion. (A)

2. A second to a motion signifies that at least two people:
   A. want the motion to be adopted.
   B. want the motion to be considered.
   C. will speak in favor of the motion.
   D. will debate the motion.
   E. will not oppose the motion. (B)

3. In taking the vote on a motion, the chair should first:
   A. take the affirmative vote.
   B. take the negative vote.
   C. announce the vote that will be required for adoption.
   D. restate the motion.
   E. ask if there are any abstentions. (D)

4. A main motion can be introduced:
   A. at any time.
   B. whenever a majority will allow its introduction.
   C. whenever the chair feels that it is appropriate.
   D. only when no privileged motions are pending.
   E. only when no other business is pending. (E)

5. Motions that can be applied to a main motion include:
   A. all privileged motions.
   B. all subsidiary motions.
   C. all privileged and subsidiary motions.
   D. all motions.
   E. none of the above. (B)

Lesson 6: Resolutions

1. The correct procedure for amending and adopting resolutions is:
   A. amend the preamble; amend the resolving clauses; vote on the entire resolution as amended.
   B. amend the resolving clauses; amend the preamble; vote on the entire resolution as amended.
   C. amend the resolving clauses; vote only on the resolving clauses.
   D. amend the preamble; amend the resolving clauses; vote only on the resolving clauses.
   E. amend the resolving clauses; vote on the entire resolution as amended. (B)

2. When a resolution is being amended, editorial or number changes should be:
   A. discouraged.
   B. prohibited.
   C. made by the secretary.
   D. made by the executive board.
   E. approved by the mover of the resolution. (C)

3. Resolutions may be presented:
   A. only by individuals.
   B. only by committees.
   C. only by the chair.
   D. either by individuals or committees.
   E. either by committees or the chair. (D)

Lesson 7: The Amending Process

1. A hostile amendment is defined as an amendment that:
   A.   is not germane to the main motion.
   B.   is not in accord with the intent of the original motion.
   C.   inserts the word "not" into the original motion.
   D.   censures the maker of the original motion.
   E.   is designed to defeat the original motion.   (B)

2. *AIPSC* recommends that, when blanks are to be filled:
   A.   members vote "Aye" or "No" on each proposal until one proposal receives a majority vote.
   B.   each member votes for one proposal, and the proposal receiving the largest number of votes be inserted into the blank.
   C.   the chair take a counted vote on all proposals, and the proposal receiving the largest majority be inserted into the blank.
   D.   the chair take a voice vote on all proposals, and the proposal receiving the largest number of affirmative votes be inserted into the blank.
   E.   the chair use the general consent procedure.   (C)

3. A type of amendment that is always out of order is:
   A.   friendly.
   B.   hostile.
   C.   primary.
   D.   secondary.
   E.   tertiary.   (E)

4. The chair should rule out of order any amendment that is:
   A.   friendly.
   B.   hostile.
   C.   not in accord with the intent of the original motion.
   D.   not germane to the motion to which it is applied.
   E.   not accepted by the maker of the motion.   (D)

5. A member moves to amend the main motion "to raise our dues from $25 to $35 per year" by striking out "year" and inserting "month." The chair should:
   A.   rule the amendment out of order as dilatory.
   B.   adopt the amendment by general consent.
   C.   ask the mover if the amendment is acceptable.
   D.   ask if there is a motion to create a blank.
   E.   state the question on the amendment.   (E)

6. Amendments are:
   A. always debatable.
   B. never debatable.
   C. debatable only if the motion to which they apply is debatable.
   D. debatable only if applied to an amendable motion.
   E. debatable only if applied to a primary amendment. (C)

7. An amendment that repeats a previously adopted motion is:
   A. dilatory.
   B. improper.
   C. not germane to the pending motion.
   D. friendly.
   E. hostile. (B)

8. A substitute motion that replaces the entire text of the main motion with alternative text is a:
   A. primary amendment.
   B. secondary amendment.
   C. tertiary amendment.
   D. friendly amendment.
   E. hostile amendment. (A)

9. According to *RONR*, when a substitute motion is introduced:
   A. only the original motion may be amended.
   B. only the substitute may be amended.
   C. both the original motion and the substitute may be amended.
   D. neither the original motion nor the substitute may be amended.
   E. it is neither amendable nor debatable. (C)

Lesson 8: Precedence of Motions and Table of Motions

1. Motions designed to expedite or dispose of the pending motion, other than to adopt or reject, it are called:
   A. privileged motions.
   B. subsidiary motions.
   C. incidental motions.
   D. incidental main motions.
   E. main motions. (B)

2. The principle of precedence states that motions are:
   A. introduced from the lowest to the highest rank but are disposed of from the highest to the lowest rank.
   B. introduced from the highest to the lowest rank but are disposed of from the lowest to the highest rank.
   C. introduced from the lowest to the highest rank and disposed of in the same order.
   D. introduced from the highest to the lowest rank and disposed of in the same order.
   E. voted on the same order that they are proposed. (A)

3. The only motions listed by *AIPSC* as reconsiderable are:
   A. privileged motions.
   B. subsidiary motions.
   C. privileged and subsidiary motions.
   D. all subsidiary motions except lay on the table and the privileged motions to adjourn.
   E. main motions. (E)

4. The motion to fix a time to which to adjourn provides for:
   A. the hour of adjournment for the same meeting.
   B. the hour of adjournment for a future meeting.
   C. a future time to continue the same meeting.
   D. a future time to call the next regular meeting.
   E. continuation of the meeting until a specified time. (C)

5. Which of the following is in order while a motion to postpone to a certain time is pending?
   A. a main motion.
   B. a motion for the previous question.
   C. a motion to postpone indefinitely.
   D. a motion to amend the main motion.
   E. a motion to refer to a committee. (B)

Lesson 9: Subsidiary Motions

1. The proper use of the motion to lay on the table is to:
    A. set aside pending matters in order to take care of some emergency.
    B. set aside a pending motion temporarily when the assembly appears unprepared to make a decision.
    C. dispose of a main motion without bringing the motion to a direct vote.
    D. test the support for a main motion before the motion is brought to a vote.
    E. set aside pending business until a future meeting.   (A)

2. A motion to create an ad hoc committee, moved while no other motion is pending:
    A. a privileged motion.
    B. the subsidiary motion to commit.
    C. a motion to create a special order of business.
    D. an incidental motion.
    E. a main motion.   (E)

3. According to *RONR*, the only motion that is intended to kill the main motion is the motion to:
    A. lay on the table.
    B. postpone to a certain time.
    C. postpone indefinitely.
    D. refer to a committee.
    E. reconsider.   (C)

4. A motion to place limitations on debate for all or a portion of an entire meeting or session is:
    A. the subsidiary motion to limit debate.
    B. the privileged motion to limit debate.
    C. an undebatable incidental motion.
    D. a debatable incidental main motion.
    E. a standing rule.   (D)

5. Which of the following takes precedence over all subsidiary motions except the motion to lay on the table?
    A. refer to a committee.
    B. postpone indefinitely.
    C. postpone to a certain time.
    D. previous question.
    E. limit debate.   (D)

6. One of the purposes of the motion for the previous question is to:
    A. adjourn the meeting.
    B. prevent further motions.
    C. prevent further amendments.
    D. prevent the meeting from adjourning until all business on the adopted agenda has been completed.
    E. require the chair to return to the regularly scheduled order of business.   (C)

7. A motion that must specify the time at which the main question will again be taken up is:
    A. lay on the table.
    B. refer to a committee.
    C. reconsider.
    D. postpone indefinitely.
    E. postpone to a certain time.   (E)

8. Amendments are debatable:
    A. in all cases.
    B. only when applied to privileged motions.
    C. only when applied to main motions.
    D. only when applied to debatable motions.
    E. only when applied to motions requiring a two-thirds vote.   (D)

9. Amendments to pending motions are adopted by majority vote:
    A. in all cases.
    B. unless applied to undebatable motions.
    C. unless applied to motions requiring a two-thirds vote.
    D. unless applied to privileged motions.
    E. in no cases; amendments always require a two-thirds vote.   (A)

10. If a matter is postponed until the next session:
    A. it should be introduced as new business at the next session.
    B. it should be introduced as a general order at the next session.
    C. it should be taken from the table at the next session.
    D. it should be reconsidered at the next session.
    E. the agenda should be amended at the next session to make it a special order of business.   (B)

Lesson 10: Privileged Motions

1. If a motion to adjourn is moved and seconded, and the chair is aware of important business requiring attention before adjournment, the chair should:
    A. refuse to state the question on the motion to adjourn.
    B. immediately order a quorum count.
    C. immediately state the question and take the vote on the motion to adjourn.
    D. inform the members of the important business before taking the vote on the motion to adjourn.
    E. ask for a motion to postpone all pending business to the next meeting. (D)

2. The business of an adjourned meeting consists of:
    A. only reading and approval of the minutes of the previous meeting.
    B. a continuation of business from the exact point at which the previous meeting adjourned.
    C. reading and approval of the minutes, followed by a continuation of business from the point at which the previous meeting adjourned.
    D. only the business that was stated in the call of the meeting.
    E. reconsideration of any motions that were adopted at the previous meeting, followed by a continuation of business from the point at which the previous meeting adjourned. (C)

3. The privileged motion to adjourn can be proposed:
    A. only while other motions are pending.
    B. only while no other motions are pending.
    C. only when all business on the adopted agenda has been disposed of.
    D. at any time following committee reports.
    E. at any time except when another has the floor. (E)

4. A motion to adjourn that is moved when there is no provision to meet again should be processed as:
    A. a main motion.
    B. an incidental motion.
    C. a privileged motion.
    D. a dilatory motion.
    E. an improper motion. (A)

5.   Raising a question of privilege requires:
      A.   a two-thirds vote for adoption.
      B.   a majority vote for adoption.
      C.   no vote, as it is ruled on by the chair.
      D.   two votes, one to bring the matter before the assembly, and another vote to adopt the motion.
      E.   previous notice and a two-thirds vote for adoption.   (C)

Lesson 11: Incidental Motions

1. When an appeal from the decision of the chair is pending, the chair should put the question by saying:
   A. Shall the appeal be sustained?
   B. Shall the chair be sustained?
   C. Shall the decision of the chair be sustained?
   D. Shall the ruling of the Chair stand as the ruling of the assembly?
   E. Shall the appeal stand as the ruling of the assembly?   (C)

2. According to *AIPSC*, when a proposal is pending and members need greater freedom in regard to the rules of debate, the preferred motion is:
   A. committee of the whole.
   B. quasi committee of the whole.
   C. informal consideration.
   D. suspend the rules.
   E. consider seriatim.   (C)

3. When the vote is taken on an appeal, a tie vote:
   A. sustains the decision of the chair.
   B. sustain the appeal.
   C. permits the chair to vote to break the tie.
   D. is indecisive and a second vote must be taken.
   E. is entered into the minutes as an indecisive vote.   (A)

4. When a demand for a division of the assembly is made, the chair should:
   A. take a voice vote.
   B. take a standing vote.
   C. take a ballot vote.
   D. ask for a second to the motion.
   E. require the mover to restate the motion in the affirmative.   (B)

5. The vote required to close or reopen nominations is:
   A. a majority vote.
   B. a two-thirds vote.
   C. a two-thirds vote with previous notice.
   D. a majority vote to close nominations and a two-thirds vote to reopen nominations.
   E. a two-thirds vote to close nominations and a majority vote to reopen nominations.   (E)

6.   A parliamentary inquiry is defined as:
      A.   a demand that the rules of the assembly be followed.
      B.   a demand that parliamentary information be distributed.
      C.   a request for substantive information about a pending motion.
      D.   a request for information about the rules of parliamentary
            procedure.
      E.   a request for more time to debate a pending motion.   (D)

7.   When a debatable appeal is pending, the chair may enter into debate:
      A.   without any limit on the number of speeches allowed.
      B.   only once, after leaving the chair.
      C.   only once, while remaining in the chair.
      D.   twice, after leaving the chair.
      E.   twice, while remaining in the chair.   (E)

8.   When an objection to consideration is pending, the chair should say:
      A.   What is the reason for this objection?
      B.   Is there a second to the motion?
      C.   Shall the objection be sustained?
      D.   Shall the question be considered?
      E.   The motion is withdrawn.   (D)

9.   The required vote to suspend a rule of parliamentary procedure is:
      A.   a majority vote.
      B.   a two-thirds vote.
      C.   a unanimous vote.
      D.   any two members who request the suspension.
      E.   none of the above.   (B)

10.   The motion to consider seriatim is appropriate for:
      A.   short, simple motions.
      B.   lengthy, complex motions.
      C.   motions that require more than a majority vote.
      D.   motions to amend the bylaws.
      E.   motions that are not amendable.   (B)

Lesson 12: Changing Previous Decisions

1. Unless a motion to take from the table is adopted, a motion that has been laid on the table remains there:
   A.   indefinitely.
   B.   until the conclusion of the same session.
   C.   until the beginning of the next session.
   D.   until the end of the next session.
   E.   until the chair announces it as an item of new business.   (D)

2. If the motion to ratify an action taken by a committee is defeated:
   A.   the action taken by the committee is nullified.
   B.   the society assumes liability for the committee's action.
   C.   the motion to ratify should be reconsidered.
   D.   those who took the action are fully responsible for the results.
   E.   disciplinary proceedings should be commenced against those who took the action.   (D)

3. *AIPSC* permits application of the motion to rescind:
   A.   to any main or subsidiary motion.
   B.   to any main or secondary motion.
   C.   only to main motions that have not been reconsidered.
   D.   only to main motions that were improperly adopted.
   E.   only to main motions.   (E)

4. The motion to amend a motion already adopted can be applied to:
   A.   any motion.
   B.   any adopted motion.
   C.   any adopted main motion.
   D.   any part of an adopted main motion that has been acted on.
   E.   any part of an adopted main motion that has not been carried out.   (E)

5. Specific main motions are in order:
   A.   at any time.
   B.   during new business.
   C.   during unfinished business.
   D.   when no business is pending.
   E.   when the chair announces that specific main motions are in order.   (D)

Lesson 13: The Presiding Officer: President – Chair

1 When a member makes a motion that contains confusing and contradictory wording, the chair should:
   A. rule the motion out of order.
   B. refuse to state the question until the motion is amended.
   C. ask if there are amendments to the motion.
   D. help the member rephrase the motion.
   E. object to consideration of the question.   (D)

2. A motion for the previous question is moved while a motion to lay on the table is pending. The chair should:
   A. rule the motion for the previous question not in order.
   B. rule the motion to lay on the table not in order.
   C. state the question on the motion for the previous question.
   D. state the question on the motion to lay on the table.
   E. ignore both motions, and proceed to the next item of business on the agenda.   (A)

Lesson 14: Debate

1. An occupant of the chair who wishes to debate a pending motion should:
    A. enter into debate while presiding.
    B. not enter into debate under any circumstances.
    C. ask the assembly to elect a temporary chair.
    D. call on the next officer in rank to preside during the rest of the debate on the motion.
    E. call on the next officer in rank to preside during the rest of the meeting. (D)

2. According to *RONR*, the effect of adopting the motion for informal consideration is to:
    A. close debate.
    B. recess the assembly to allow for caucus meetings.
    C. extend the time limits for debate on a motion.
    D. allow an unlimited number of speeches by any member.
    E. allow the chair to enter into debate on the pending motion. (D)

3. According to *RONR*, two undebatable motions are:
    A. limit debate and reconsider.
    B. recess and ratify.
    C. previous question and object to consideration.
    D. object to consideration and postpone indefinitely.
    E. previous question and appeal from the ruling of the chair. (C)

4. While a member A is speaking, member B rises to a request for information. According to *AIPSC*, the chair should:
    A. refuse to allow the request for information until member A is finished speaking.
    B. direct member A to respond to the request for information at once.
    C. direct member A to respond to the question after he is finished with his remarks.
    D. ask member A if he is willing to respond at once, with the response being deducted from his speaking time.
    E. ask member A if he is willing to respond at once, with no deduction from his speaking time. (E)

Lesson 15: Strategy of Debate

1. If personalities are likely to influence the vote on a motion, the best strategy is to:
    A. rise to a point of order.
    B. rise to a request for information.
    C. move to refer to a committee.
    D. object to consideration.
    E. move for a ballot vote. (E)

2. *RONR* is the parliamentary authority, and a member who favors adoption of a main motion believes that the motion will be defeated. A good strategy is to:
    A. vote with the prevailing side.
    B. vote with the minority.
    C. abstain.
    D. plan to renew the motion during the same meeting.
    E. move to close debate. (A)

Lesson 16: Quorum

1. Unless otherwise defined in the bylaws, a quorum at a convention is a majority of:
   A. the registered delegates and others qualified to vote who are present.
   B. the registered delegates and others qualified to vote whether or not they are present.
   C. all voting and nonvoting delegates.
   D. the registered delegates who participate in voting.
   E. all voting and nonvoting delegates who are reported by the credentials committee. (B)

2. The purpose of a quorum requirement is to ensure that:
   A. all voting members are present for important decisions.
   B. those responsible for implementing decisions are present.
   C. a small minority is not allowed to make decisions.
   D. the majority is not allowed to dominate the minority.
   E. proper notice of the meeting is distributed to all members. (C)

3. Quorum always refers to:
   A. members present.
   B. members present and voting.
   C. members and guest present.
   D. the total number of members in good standing.
   E. the number of members required to adopt a motion. (A)

Lesson 17: Minutes

1. The most common method of approving minutes is by:
   A. majority vote.
   B. two-thirds vote.
   C. unanimous or general consent.
   D. the motion to amend something previously adopted.
   E. the motion to reconsider and enter on the minutes.   (C)

2. Minutes should be erased from the minutes book:
   A. when a motion to rescind or expunge is adopted.
   B. whenever an adopted motion has been fully implemented
   C. when it is obvious that an error has been made.
   D. whenever a motion is adopted to amend the minutes.
   E. never.   (E)

3. The minutes of a meeting should not include:
   A. the name of the mover of a main motion.
   B. the name of the seconder of a main motion.
   C. the result of a vote on a main motion.
   D. points of order and appeals.
   E. counted votes for each side.   (B)

Lesson 18: Finances

1. The appropriate action for an assembly to take on an auditor's report is:
   A. adopt it by majority vote.
   B. adopt it by a two-thirds vote.
   C. receive it and place it on file.
   D. refer it to the treasurer.
   E. refer it to the finance committee. (A)

2. The finance committee may not:
   A. submit a budget to the assembly for its approval.
   B. advise on ways to help finance authorized projects.
   C. make recommendations regarding financial transactions.
   D. make purchases or execute financial transactions.
   E. review bylaws and standing rules for financial obligations. (D)

3. The purpose of an audit is to:
   A. assist the treasurer in preparing his report.
   B. authorize the expenditure of funds.
   C. inform the assembly regarding sources of income and disbursements.
   D. verify the accuracy of the treasurer's report.
   E. verify the competence of the treasurer. (D)

4. The treasurer should pay bills:
   A. when authorized by the finance committee.
   B. when authorized by the auditors.
   C. whenever legitimate bills are presented that can be verified in the adopted budget.
   D. when authorized by vote of the membership or board, as stated in the bylaws.
   E. as soon as it is determined that there are sufficient funds available to make payment. (D)

Lesson 19: Officers

1. The president often serves as an ex officio member of all committees except:
   A. the finance committee.
   B. the bylaws committee.
   C. the nominating committee.
   D. the rules committee.
   E. reference committees. (C)

2. At each regular meeting, the treasurer should present a report which contains:
   A. the amount on hand at the previous meeting, receipts, disbursements, and the amount currently on hand.
   B. the amount on hand at the previous meeting and the amount currently on hand.
   C. receipts and disbursements since the previous meeting and the amount currently on hand.
   D. only the amount currently on hand.
   E. an update of all items stated in the adopted budget. (A)

3. The secretary:
   A. participates in business meetings only when someone else is assigned to take the minutes.
   B. has the same right as any other member to participate in business meetings.
   C. is required to participate fully in all business meetings.
   D. participates only in the business of executive sessions.
   E. never participates in business meetings. (B)

Lesson 20: Executive Board or Board of Directors

1. During meetings of small boards, the chair, if a member, should:
    A. remain completely impartial regarding all business that comes before the board.
    B. feel free to make motions, enter into debate, and vote.
    C. enter into debate, but refrain from voting on motions.
    D. vote on motions, but refrain from participating in debate.
    E. propose and debate motions, but refrain from voting.   (B)

2. A small board is defined by *RONR* as:
    A. twenty or fewer members.
    B. twelve or fewer members.
    C. six or fewer members.
    D. three or fewer members.
    E. any number smaller than the general assembly.   (B)

3. Unless otherwise stated in the bylaws, a quorum of a board is:
    A. the full membership of the board.
    B. two-thirds of the members of the board.
    C. a majority of the members of the board.
    D. the members present.
    E. at least two officers and the members present.   (C)

4. Unfinished business of an outgoing board:
    A. must be attended to at the final meeting.
    B. automatically becomes new business for the next board.
    C. becomes unfinished business for the next board.
    D. is terminated with that administration.
    E. is laid on the table.   (D)

5. An executive committee reports:
    A. to the assembly.
    B. to the board.
    C. only in meetings of the executive committee.
    D. only in executive session of the board.
    E. during the organization's annual meeting.   (B)

6. In small boards, the chair should:
    A. refrain from making motions.
    B. not vote on motions.
    C. not discuss motions without leaving the chair.
    D. not require that motions be seconded.
    E. rise while putting motions to a vote.   (D)

Lesson 21: Membership

1. Ultimate control of a volunteer organization belongs to:
    A.   the officers.
    B.   the board of directors.
    C.   the members.
    D.   the parent organization.
    E.   society.   (C)

2. Before joining an organization, a prospective member should:
    A.   serve as parliamentarian for the organization.
    B.   run for office in the organization.
    C.   serve on one or more committees of the organization.
    D.   read the organization's bylaws.
    E.   vote in an election of the organization.   (D)

3. According to *RONR*, which motion requires only a majority vote for adoption?
    A.   Adopt bylaws amendments.
    B.   Limit debate.
    C.   Close nominations.
    D.   Suspend the rules.
    E.   Division of a question.   (E)

Lesson 22: Committees

1   According to *RONR*, in counting a quorum of a committee, one should include:
- A.   any members of the organization who choose to attend the committee's meetings.
- B.   any of the officers or members of the executive board who attend the committee's meetings.
- C.   all members of the committee, whether or not present.
- D.   any member of the organization who is an ex officio member of the committee.
- E.   any member of the organization except the president who is an ex officio member of the committee.   (E)

2.   Which of the following cannot exist unless provided for in the bylaws?
- A.   A standing committee.
- B.   A special committee.
- C.   A nominating committee.
- D.   An ad hoc committee.
- E.   An executive committee.   (E)

3.   Committees that are usually provided for in the bylaws are:
- A.   standing committees
- B.   ad hoc committees.
- C.   committees to investigate.
- D.   committees to recommend action.
- E.   committees to take action.   (A)

4.   According to *RONR*, which of the following motions is out of order in committees?
- A.   Reconsider.
- B.   Close debate.
- C.   Postpone to a certain time.
- D.   Recess.
- E.   Adjourn.   (B)

5.   A special committee dissolves when:
- A.   the committee chair determines that the committee's work is finished.
- B.   the committee adopts a motion to dissolve.
- C.   the presiding officer of the assembly discharges the committee.
- D.   the committee cannot obtain a quorum at meetings.
- E.   the committee makes its final report to the assembly.   (E)

6. The most common committee officers are:
   A. a chair, a vice chair, a secretary, and a treasurer.
   B. a chair, a vice chair, and a secretary.
   C. a chair, a vice chair, and a treasurer.
   D. a chair and a vice chair.
   E. a chair and a secretary. (E)

7. A subcommittee reports to:
   A. the executive committee.
   B. the appointing committee.
   C. the assembly.
   D. the board of directors.
   E. the president. (B)

Lesson 23: Committee Reports

1. When a committee report has been presented to the organization, the report is said to have been:
   A. accepted.
   B. adopted.
   C. received.
   D. endorsed.
   E. approved. (C)

2. A committee's recommendations should usually be placed:
   A. at the beginning of the committee report.
   B. in the middle of the committee report.
   C. at the end of the committee report.
   D. in a separate motion rather than as part of the report.
   E. in a standing rule. (C)

3. A committee report should be signed by:
   A. the committee chair.
   B. all of the members of the committee.
   C. all of the members of the committee who attended all of the meetings.
   D. all of the members of the committee who concur with the report.
   E. a quorum of the committee. (D)

4. The usual reporting member of a committee is:
   A. the chair.
   B. the vice chair.
   C. the secretary.
   D. a spokesman for those who concur with the report.
   E. any member of the committee, selected at random. (A)

5. A minority report should be presented:
   A. immediately before the committee report is presented.
   B. immediately following presentation of the committee report.
   C. during consideration of the committee report.
   D. following the assembly's action on the committee report.
   E. under the heading of unfinished business. (B)

6.   If members of the assembly wish to act on a minority report, the minority report is processed as:
   A.   a main motion.
   B.   an amendment by striking out and inserting.
   C.   a motion to substitute.
   D.   a motion to amend something previously adopted.
   E.   a dissenting opinion, offered for information only.   (C)

Lesson 24: Bylaws, Part I

1. Which of the following articles should normally be placed last in the bylaws?
    A. Parliamentary Authority.
    B. Meetings.
    C. Elections.
    D. Committees.
    E. Amendment. (E)

2. The first five articles of a set of bylaws, listed in order, should be:
    A. Name, Object/Purpose, Officers, Membership, Meetings.
    B. Name, Object/Purpose, Membership, Officers, Meetings.
    C. Name, Object/Purpose, Membership, Meetings, Officers.
    D. Name, Object/Purpose, Officers, Board of Directors, Membership.
    E. Name, Object/Purpose, Officers, Board of Directors, Meetings.(B)

3. When writing bylaws, one should include information regarding dues or fees in the article on:
    A. committees.
    B. finances.
    C. membership.
    D. officers.
    E. discipline. (C)

4. When writing bylaws, one should include information regarding the quorum in the article on:
    A. meetings.
    B. officers.
    C. parliamentary authority.
    D. amendments.
    E. elections. (A)

Lesson 25: Bylaws, Part II

1. According to *RONR*, the usual requirement for amending bylaws is:
    A. a two-thirds vote.
    B. two-thirds of the total membership.
    C. previous notice and a two-thirds vote.
    D. previous notice and a vote of two-thirds of the total membership.
    E. unanimous consent.   (C)

2. The vote required to adopt an amendment to a proposed bylaw amendment is:
    A. a majority vote.
    B. a two-thirds vote.
    C. a two-thirds vote with previous notice.
    D. a vote of two-thirds of the total membership with previous notice.
    E. the same as the vote required to adopt the bylaw amendment.(A)

3. When adopting a revision of the bylaws, the group should have the entire revision open to discussion:
    A. immediately following the report of the bylaws committee.
    B. as soon as the chair has stated the question on adopting the revision.
    C. after each article in the revision has been discussed and refined by amendment.
    D. at any time during consideration of the revision.
    E. after the final vote has been taken on the revision.   (C)

4. A motion to dissolve a society is, in effect, a motion:
    A. to rescind the bylaws.
    B. to amend something previously adopted.
    C. to revoke the society's charter.
    D. that is considered illegal in most states.
    E. to create a new society.   (A)

5. Previous notice of a revision of the bylaws:
    A. must include notice of each proposed change in the bylaws.
    B. must be mailed to each member of the organization.
    C. must be announced at least three meetings prior to the consideration of the revision.
    D. should include a copy of the proposed revision and when the revision will be considered.
    E. is never required.   (D)

Lesson 26: Standing Rules

1. According to *RONR*, custom has the effect of:
   A. bylaws.
   B. a main motion that has a continuing effect until amended or rescinded.
   C. a standing rule that may be discontinued by majority vote with notice.
   D. a standing rule that may be discontinued by majority vote without notice.
   E. a standing rule that may be discontinued by a two-thirds vote without notice. (D)

2. Most organizations adopt standing rules:
   A. at the annual meeting.
   B. at the beginning of each new session.
   C. at the beginning of each meeting.
   D. that apply to each meeting and continue from meeting to meeting.
   E. in the bylaws, and these rules continue until the bylaws are amended. (D)

3. Policy, which defines belief or philosophy, should be:
   A. included in the charter.
   B. included in the bylaws.
   C. included in the standing rules.
   D. stated usually as resolutions which, if adopted, are as binding as the bylaws.
   E. stated usually as resolutions which, if adopted, are as binding as the standing rules. (D)

Lesson 27: Voting Methods

1. Which of the following methods of voting cannot be used unless authorized by the bylaws or by a motion from the floor prior to taking the vote?
   A. Roll call vote.
   B. Write-in vote.
   C. Standing vote.
   D. Show of hands.
   E. Voice vote.   (A)

2. Which method of voting provides for casting all of one's votes for one nominee when several are on the ballot?
   A. Preferential voting.
   B. Cumulative voting.
   C. Bullet voting.
   D. Mail balloting.
   E. Proxy voting.   (B)

3. Which method of voting gives a member the power of attorney to vote for another member?
   A. Proxy voting.
   B. Bullet voting.
   C. Mail balloting.
   D. Cumulative voting.
   E. Preferential voting.   (A)

4. Which form of voting is useful when there is no minority whose voting rights must be protected?
   A. Majority vote.
   B. Two-thirds vote.
   C. General/unanimous consent.
   D. Proxy vote.
   E. Mail ballot.   (C)

5.   The effect of an abstention is to:
      A.   increase the number required to obtain a majority of those present and voting.
      B.   decrease the number required to obtain a majority of those present and voting.
      C.   make it more difficult for any candidate to obtain a majority vote.
      D.   increase the chances that a minority candidate will eventually be elected.
      E.   diminish the chances that the election will be declared invalid because of lack of a quorum.   (B)

6.   Write-in votes may be used:
      A.   only if provided for in the bylaws.
      B.   for any election, unless prohibited by the bylaws.
      C.   for any election in which only one candidate is nominated for an office.
      D.   only during preferential balloting.
      E.   only during cumulative voting.   (B)

Lesson 28: Nominations

1.   The motion to close nominations is:
      A.   debatable and requires a two-thirds vote.
      B.   not debatable and requires a two-thirds vote.
      C.   debatable and requires a majority vote.
      D.   not debatable and requires a majority vote.
      E.   always adopted by general consent.   (B)

2.   The most common method of making nominations, which is always in
      order unless prohibited in the bylaws, is:
      A.   nomination by the chair.
      B.   nomination from the floor.
      C.   nomination by committee.
      D.   nomination by ballot.
      E.   nomination by petition.   (B)

3.   The nominating committee is usually:
      A.   appointed by the chair.
      B.   elected by the board of directors.
      C.   established by the adoption of a main motion.
      D.   provided for in the standing rules.
      E.   provided for in the bylaws.   (E)

Lesson 29: Elections

1. When an error in counting a ballot vote is discovered:
    A. a re-ballot is taken in all cases.
    B. a re-ballot is taken only if authorized by the assembly.
    C. a re-ballot is taken only if authorized by the board of directors.
    D. a re-ballot is taken only if the error affects the result of the election.
    E. a re-ballot is never taken; however the assembly may order a recount. (D)

2. Which method of voting violates the principle of one person/one vote?
    A. Preferential voting.
    B. Cumulative voting.
    C. Bullet voting.
    D. Plurality vote.
    E. Roll call vote. (B)

3. Elections normally require:
    A. a plurality.
    B. a majority vote of the total membership.
    C. a majority vote of members present, providing that a quorum is present.
    D. a majority vote of members present and voting, providing that a quorum is present.
    E. a unanimous vote. (D)

4. Who is excluded from voting in a ballot election?
    A. The chair.
    B. The tellers.
    C. The chair and the tellers.
    D. The candidates for office.
    E. None of the above. (E)

Lesson 30: The Professional Parliamentarian

1   During a business meeting, the effective parliamentarian should normally:

    A.   become an advocate for those issues which will be of most benefit to the organization.

    B.   give rulings whenever these appear helpful.

    C.   advise on legal matters.

    D.   explain all opinions fully and provide sources for opinions given.

    E.   dispense advice to the chair as inconspicuously as possible. (E)

2.   During a business meeting, questions to the parliamentarian should be:

    A.   addressed through the chair, and answered by the parliamentarian.

    B.   addressed through the chair, and answered by the chair.

    C.   addressed through the chair, and answered either by the chair or the parliamentarian.

    D.   addressed to the parliamentarian.

    E.   discouraged, as such questions may interrupt the orderly flow of business. (C)

3.   A parliamentarian should give rulings:

    A.   whenever a controversial matter arises in the assembly.

    B.   whenever a member of the assembly requests a ruling.

    C.   only when the assembly adopts a motion requesting a ruling.

    D.   only when directed by the chair.

    E.   never. (E)

4.   Which of the following is not a required quality of a good professional parliamentarian?

    A.   Thorough understanding of the principles of parliamentary law and procedure.

    B.   Ability to assert forceful leadership on major issues confronting the organization.

    C.   Ability to write parliamentary opinions clearly and succinctly.

    D.   Patience to endure calmly any minor breaches of rules that do not affect the result.

    E.   Ability to preside at meetings of the organization. (B)

Lesson 31: Discipline

1. The effect of a motion of no confidence is to:
   A. censure the chair.
   B. prefer charges against the chair.
   C. put the chair on notice that some members disagree with the behavior of the chair while presiding.
   D. put the chair on notice that a motion to censure may be adopted if the chair's behavior is not corrected.
   E. put the organization on notice that its bylaws may need to be amended.   (C)

2. When the chair "names" an offender, this means that:
   A. the offender's name will be entered in the minutes.
   B. the offender's name will be deleted from the membership list.
   C. the offender will be removed from the assembly hall.
   D. the offender is put on notice that his behavior must be corrected or disciplinary action will follow.
   E. none of the above.   (A)

3. When an investigative committee reports its findings of misconduct, this report is given:
   A. in the open assembly meeting, after which a trial is held in executive session.
   B. in executive session, after which a trial is held in executive session.
   C. in the open assembly meeting, after which a trial is held in open assembly meeting.
   D. in executive session, after which a trial is held in open assembly meeting.
   E. to the board of directors, which then decides whether a trial should be held.   (B)

Lesson 32: Conventions

1. No convention can begin business until the reports of three committees, listed in order, have been adopted:
    A. rules, program, credentials.
    B. rules, credentials, program.
    C. credentials, rules, program.
    D. credentials, program, rules.
    E. program, credentials, rules. (C)

2. The rules committee of a convention, in preparing a set of convention rules, may:
    A. deviate from the bylaws, but not from the adopted parliamentary authority.
    B. deviate from the adopted parliamentary authority, but not from the bylaws.
    C. deviate from both the adopted parliamentary authority and from the bylaws.
    D. not deviate from either the bylaws or the adopted parliamentary authority.
    E. not deviate from the convention rules used during the previous convention. (B)

3. The task of determining who is qualified to vote at a convention is normally performed by:
    A. the program committee.
    B. the rules committee.
    C. the credentials committee.
    D. the public relations committee.
    E. the platform committee. (C)

4. The most important function of an alternate at a convention is to:
    A. serve as an advisor to elected delegates.
    B. enable delegates to take frequent coffee breaks without losing their vote.
    C. attend caucus meetings when delegates are too busy to attend.
    D. bolster the voting strength of their delegation.
    E. replace delegates who have officially departed from the convention. (E)

5. The resolutions committee does not have authority to:
    A. put duplicate resolutions into one substance, after conferring with sponsors.
    B. present resolutions to the assembly in logical sequence.
    C. adopt or reject resolutions referred to the committee.
    D. present resolutions of its own.
    E. see to it that resolutions are prepared in proper form. (C)

6. The report of a program committee of a convention:
    A. requires a unanimous vote for adoption.
    B. requires a two-thirds vote for adoption.
    C. requires a majority vote for adoption.
    D. should never be amended after it has been adopted by the assembly.
    E. should be adopted before any other committee reports are presented. (C)

7. The convention parliamentarian should be seated:
    A. next to the association attorney.
    B. at the far end of the head table.
    C. as close to the president as possible.
    D. in a special section of the room reserved for invited guests.
    E. with the delegates, preferably in the front row. (C)

8. During a convention, the proper use of microphones should be:
    A. included in the parliamentary authority.
    B. included in the convention standing rules.
    C. included in the organization's bylaws.
    D. included in the secretary's report, but not included in any documents.
    E. announced by the chair, but not included in any documents. (B)